Preacher's Proverbs

Wisdom Taught and Caught in My Life

Pastor Brad Reed

ISBN 979-8-88832-947-4 (paperback)
ISBN 979-8-88832-948-1 (digital)

Christian Faith Publishing
832 Park Avenue
Meadville, PA 16335
www.christianfaithpublishing.com

Printed in the United States of America

I would like to dedicate this book to my wonderful wife, Joleen. When we vowed before God and our families that we would stick together for better, for worse, for richer, for poorer, in sickness and in health, we were very optimistic. Who would have thought that we would face them all? Joleen, you have stood beside me, cheered me on, and at times pushed me in this life of ministry. I couldn't have made it without you. I am so thankful for my "little helper."

I also want to mention a few of the men and women of God that have invested in me: My pastor, Rev. Freddy Burcham, Rev. E. T. Kelley, Rev. Charles Cross, Sister Wanda Weaver, and my great friend with whom I spent many hours sharing and talking with, Rev. Terry Miller.

Webster's Dictionary defines a proverb as a short, traditional saying that expresses some obvious truth or familiar experience. This following book has been birthed out of different statements that have been shared with me by older ministers, which I am sure were trying to teach me some obvious truth or a truth that they felt I obviously needed to learn—some are what I have observed myself. As I sit down to write this, I apologize to you, the reader, that I am not a great writer, but then I remember one of those wise sayings my first pastor told me after I had preached my first sermon. He told me, I think with a little sadistic pleasure, "Don't apologize to the people for not being a great preacher. They will figure it out on their own."

So it is with humility, thanks to those who God has put in my life to keep me so, that I write some of the things I have learned in this wonderful experience called ministry. Some of these lessons have been life changing and have helped me face some very trying times. Some were like a slap in my face, which I could say like the old aftershave commercial, "Thanks. I needed that."

My hope is that you can laugh, learn, and maybe relate to some of my experiences. Ministry is rarely easy and never boring, but there is no greater life for those who have been called into it. I hope you can say with myself and the apostle Paul (1 Timothy 1:12 KJV), "And I thank Christ Jesus our Lord, who hath enabled me, for that he counted me faithful, putting me into the ministry."

CHAPTER 1

ALWAYS START WITH PRAYER, ALWAYS

I wish I could say that this was a lesson I learned early in my ministry. Of course, I always knew the importance of prayer. Prayer for the sick, prayer for problems, prayer for a sermon, and of course, prayer over our food—prayer was something I did when I needed to. It was not an intimate or intricate part of my life.

I could pray with the best of them. I could pray with fervency, emotion, and much feeling. I could throw in a thou, a most holy and righteous, and even a "yea verily," but prayer was not a vital part of my daily life.

When I was serving as the state youth director of the Pentecostal Church of God, we lived in a small town in Missouri named Steeleville. The main street had one four-way stop, although now I think they do have a flashing red light. As we were looking for a Christian school to send our children to, we found an independent church that had a school. My wife and I decided to visit the church on a Sunday morning, just to check them out.

When we walked in, we knew immediately that something was different here. The building seemed to almost be humming—not like a tune but like a vibration. Unlike most churches, the people weren't standing around talking, they were kneeling in the altars or in the pews, praying. Instantly you could feel the presence of God.

We were hooked! The preaching was not eloquent or done with great oratory skills but like the apostle Paul said, "In demonstration of Spirit and power" (1 Corinthians 2:4).

As we began to hear the preaching and teaching, the Holy Spirit began to convict our hearts. One particular service, the Lord began to deal strongly with me about the pride in my life. Now this hurt because I was one of the humblest people I knew. I was greatly broken before God. Something had drastically changed in my heart. My relationship with God became different, closer, and more intimate. This is what God had been wanting all along, and without knowing it, this is what I had been wanting all along too.

Prayer became totally different for me from that time on. I realized that prayer is our life flow, our connection to the Vine (John 15). It was not a chore or a drudgery; it was alive! There are times you must pray until you can pray. Keep seeking until you push through the flesh, the thoughts, and distractions.

> And it came to pass, that, as he was praying in a
> certain place, when he ceased, one of his disciples
> said unto him, Lord, teach us to pray, as John
> also taught his disciples. (Luke 11:1 KJV)

He never asked Jesus to teach us to praise or worship or teach us to preach or how to conduct a spiritual service. He asked Jesus to teach all of us to pray. This disciple realized that everything that Jesus did was covered in prayer. If we start with prayer, the praise and worship, the preaching, and the spiritual service will be a natural by-product.

I dare not step into the pulpit without the time of prayer. If you are going to be a preacher with power, you must connect to the power source in prayer. Don't do anything, whether reading the Bible or preaching to a congregation, without first consulting God.

Always start with prayer, always.

Personal experience or thoughts: _______________________________

____

____

____

____

____

____

____

____

CHAPTER 2

THE CHURCH CANNOT GROW MORE SPIRITUAL THAN THE PASTOR

This is a general rule. On one hand, there may be those in your church that may surpass you in knowledge and may be a great blessing to you. On the other hand, I promise you there will be many who think they are wiser and more spiritual than you, and, well, honestly, they won't be that much of a blessing.

The more serious point that I wish to make is this: you can't expect your people to be spiritual giants if you are not spiritual. This is a scary thought, but I have found it to be true. Just as we eventually become like our parents, our congregations eventually become like their pastor.

There have been times that I have corrected my physical children about something they are doing, and they have asked me, "But why can you do it, Daddy?" Ouch!

We preach to our people about the importance of prayer and daily Bible reading, and yet our own devotional lives are often neglected. Have you noticed that when you go to a ministers' conference at a church, all the pastors try to get the back row or as far from the front row as possible? Yet we berate and chide our people for sitting in the back. Who hasn't said, "You better get here early to get a back seat"?

My church people joke (I think) that we should change our name to "The First Church of Sarcasm." I don't have a clue as to why. It's one of those things where your wife says, "*Your* child is driving me crazy!"

The point is this: you can preach faithfulness, devotion, praise, or whatever you want, but if you aren't living this life, it seems that your congregation won't either. I call this the law of leadership. You can convince everyone around you about how pious and spiritual you are, but there is a law of sowing and reaping that will come to pass.

I can't say I understand it, but I have found that it seems as though there is a line, a boundary that your people can't pass until you have.

> Be ye followers of me, even as I also *am* of Christ.
> (1 Corinthians 11:1 KJV)

Preacher, you set the standard.

Personal experience or thoughts: _______________________
____
____
____
____
____
____
____
____
____

CHAPTER 3

IF EVERYONE IN THIS CHURCH WERE JUST LIKE ME, WHAT KIND OF CHURCH WOULD THIS CHURCH BE?

This was a sign that hung over the door in the little Pentecostal church where I was saved. At the end of every service as we would slowly make our way to the exit, shaking hands and truly enjoying one another's company, I would see that sign hanging there. It was put there by one of the former pastors years before, but it has stuck with me ever since.

It seems we all know what the perfect Christian is supposed to be, and of course we are always ready to share our opinion. We love to point out everyone else's shortcomings, but we are completely oblivious to our own. I think I remember a story in the Bible about beams and motes.

The truth is that we have enough areas in our own lives needing work, that we shouldn't have much time to find fault in our church family.

I read that sign every service, that meant Sunday morning, Sunday evening, Wednesday evening, youth service, rallies, revivals, and fellowship meetings. I read it often, and it stuck with me. I began to ask myself that question. I reasoned if everyone in my church were just like me, would it be a good church? My first thought was, *It would be great*, but as I stated in a previous chapter, I have learned to be humbler. Seriously, would it be the kind of church I would want to be part of? Would there be people there every service? Would there be money in the account to meet the needs of the ministries? Would there be new converts? Would the church have a good reputation in the community? The list could almost be endless.

The point is, a great church starts with me, the individual. If I will become what I am supposed to be, then and only then can I help others. It reminds me of this old song we used to sing.

> Have thine own way Lord, have thine own way.
> Thou art the potter, I am the clay.
> Mold me and make me, after thy will.
> While I am waiting, yielded and still.

Personal experience or thoughts: _______________________

____

____

____

____

____

____

____

____

____

CHAPTER 4

YOUR FAMILY IS YOUR FIRST MINISTRY

I cannot express this strongly enough. There have been so many families sacrificed on the altar of ministry. So many marriages were destroyed because of a minister who thought the church was more important than his home or that he was above temptation.

I am saddened when I think of so many of the young ministers that I started out with that are no longer in ministry, their families are broken, and some no longer even profess Christ as their Savior.

Did they start out to fail? No, but they accepted the teaching that God and ministry are one and the same. I thank God for the calling on my life, but I had to come to the knowledge that ministry and God are not the same. Now some will disagree, and some will say, "That's the problem with the church today." Oh well.

We must learn priorities. First, we shall love the Lord, our God, with all our hearts, mind, and strength. God must be number one in our lives. Our relationship with Him is paramount. If that relationship isn't right, no other relationship will be.

When the apostle Paul was instructing pastor Timothy about bishops and deacons, he said this, "One that ruleth well his own house, having his children in subjection with all gravity; (For if a man know not how to rule his own house, how shall he take care of the church of God?) (1 Timothy 3:4–5).

The minister's family has needs and struggles that other families do not have. They have to always be perfect; the house has to be open and ready for guest at any given moment. Your children will be the example for every other child in church.

You must make sure your family is taken care of. You must make time for them. Become the pastor of the home first. Be real with your children. You can take off the church clothes when you get home, but don't let your family think that you have a split personality. You may get chuckles from making fun of your spouse from the platform, but remember he/she is probably only smiling on the outside.

I was talking to a wonderful saintly lady who was once a pastor's wife. She was one of those that, if you looked in the dictionary beside the word *Christian*, *holy*, or *consecrated*, you would see her picture. I have heard testimonies of her love for God and how great of a pastor's wife she was. One day, she shared with me her one regret in her years of service. She said that she wished she had missed a youth rally or a fellowship meeting to go watch her son play football. I will insert here that I believe that church should be a priority and the reason to miss some of the other events. Spending time with your family at church worshipping God is paramount. In this dear saint's life, she had never attended even one of his games. You can call it dedication or commitment to the ministry, but when all was said and done, she regretted that one thing.

There is a verse in the Bible that may not directly apply, but it says, "What shall a man give in exchange for his soul, and what does it profit if he shall gain the whole world and lose his own soul?" I apply that to my family. What good does it do when I face the end of my time here, and people say, "We never had a pastor that worked as hard as Pastor Reed," if my own family doesn't know me or worse, they become bitter against God and the ministry for robbing them of their father? I am going to do everything in my power to take my family to heaven with me.

As you can tell, this is an area that is near to my heart. I started out thinking like so many. It was noble to sacrifice for the ministry. Thankfully, my eyes and heart were opened. My family has still faced great pains and challenges, but because of relationships that had been a priority, we came through them. At the time of this writing, all my children are active in ministry. No plaque or accolades from a congregation or organization can compare to that.

I understand, and you need to also, that the ministry is not an occupation that you can clock out on. There will be emergencies, late night calls, and responsibilities. What I am saying is make your family a priority. Take your wife out for a special evening or a weekend getaway and spend time with your children. Make an investment in your family. How many preachers will spend money for books, CDs, or conferences (and those are important), but won't spend money on a weekend trip with their spouse or children? Make an investment! Make memories, good ones. You don't want to be looking at family pictures and say, "That was me preaching that weekend retreat," while your child says, "That was the weekend of my ninth birthday when you promised to take me camping." Things happen, and there are always schedules; just don't forget to put your family at the top. Once my wife and I had planned a much-needed vacation. The reservations were made, and the hotel was paid for. A person related to one of our members passed away unexpectedly. I really wrestled with what to do as the funeral was scheduled right in the middle of our planned vacation. After much prayer, I realized that I wasn't the only one who could handle the services. I explained to the family the best that I could and laid out the entire service to my assistant pastor. He took care of it and gained some great experience. The family was thankful that everything was taken care of, and we took our vacation. God gives us grace for more than just salvation.

I have found that my children may make faces and comments if my wife and I kiss in front of them, but they like it. It lets them know Mom and Dad are okay, and they find security in that. The same is true of the church. They need to know that the pastor and his family are okay. This has been my priority list for some time now: God, family, and ministry.

Personal experience or thoughts: _______________________________

____

____

____

____

____

____

____

____

CHAPTER 5

LIVE WHAT YOU PREACH, PREACH WHAT YOU LIVE

This has been one of those thoughts that has been with me since very early on in my Christian experience. I don't remember if this was something that was told me directly or something I learned from watching others.

Consistency is so very vital in ministry. As far as that goes in our Christian walk, I have found that not everyone sees things the way I do, and unbelievably, some may downright disagree with me, but I hope they know that I am consistent. I strive to be the same every day, in my core beliefs, my values, and my convictions.

It really used to bother me but has now become humorous when I see a preacher who sits like a knot on a log (as we say in the country), unmoved by the songs, unresponsive to other speakers, but as soon as they are introduced, look out! They come alive and preach like a house on fire (again, a country term). What is even better is when they begin preaching something along the line of, "If you don't praise the Lord, the very rocks will cry out!"

Sometimes we preachers are our own worst enemies.

If you aren't going to live it, don't tell everyone else to. I've heard preachers preach on the evils of a particular subject, only to see them involved in the same thing. I realize we do grow, and we do change. What was once wickedness, like playing softball, is now accepted, and I am not telling you what to preach, but if you are going to preach it, live it.

When you flesh out your sermons, your congregation will follow you and respect you. If you are preaching one thing and living another, no matter how good you deliver the message, you lose the impact because they know you don't believe or exercise it yourself.

> So do and observe whatever they tell you, but not
> the works they do. For they preach and do not
> practice. (Matthew 23:3 ESV)

There are ministers that I know who may not have the same convictions that I have or who may use different methods. Even though I may not agree completely with them or feel the same way about their methods, if they are consistent, I can and will respect their convictions. Religion tries to make us all exactly alike; relationships are unique to the individual.

Personal experience or thoughts: _______________

____

____

____

____

____

____

____

____

CHAPTER 6

DON'T PREACH WHAT YOU THINK, PREACH WHAT YOU KNOW

Opinions are like fingerprints; everyone has them, but no two are exactly alike.

Early on in my ministry, and well, my Christian walk, I read and heard many stories that were told as true. I would almost make a doctrine out of stories. There was the one about the missionary's son listening to rock music on his radio (the time before TikTok). An old former witch doctor heard it and asked the missionary why his son was calling up demonic spirits. The drumbeat was exactly the same as the one he had used to conjure up demons. Now I realize that many of the popular culture songs have questionable lyrics and are inspired by a spirit contrary to God's, but I'm not sure that story is true. It was, however, a great one to tell to young people at a youth rally!

One day, I was listening to the radio, and the preacher came on talking about when Jonathan, Saul's son, tasted the honey before he was supposed to, and his eyes were enlightened, as if it were a good thing or a wonderful revelation from God! The truth of the story was that King Saul had made an oath that whoever ate anything before the battle was over, should be put to death. So, the enlightening was to something not so good for Jonathan. This preacher was saying that if you will send a love offering of $10 or more, he would send you a packet of prayer blessed honey, and your eyes would be enlightened just like Jonathan's. I think the only thing being lightened would be your wallet.

We find scriptures that seem like a new revelation, but make sure that, before you change your doctrine or start criticizing your fellow ministers for not jumping on board, there is more than one verse that supports your discovery. Scripture proves scripture. Out of the mouth of two or three witnesses', things are settled.

I cannot express strongly enough that you study the Bible. Don't search the scriptures to prove your opinion or belief, but study to determine your belief. If you cannot get a formal education, get an informal one. Remember, ignorance is no excuse for stupidity.

> For the word of God *is* quick, and powerful, and sharper than any twoedged sword, piercing even to the dividing asunder of soul and spirit, and of the joints and marrow, and *is* a discerner of the thoughts and intents of the heart. (Hebrews 4:12 KJV)

Personal experience or thoughts: _______________________

____

____

____

____

____

____

____

____

CHAPTER 7

PREACH THE WORD

Allow me to share my testimony of God's calling on my life. I had been saved for a few years, had taught Sunday school, and led the youth group for a couple of years. I loved my pastor, Freddy Burcham. He was very instrumental to me being saved. I remember hoping that God would call me into the ministry, even though I really didn't know what that meant. I began to spend more time with Bro. Burcham and see more what ministry was all about. Believe it or not, it's more than preaching a couple of sermons a week! I changed my mind and my prayer. I would be happy helping in any way I could but not to preach or pastor.

One Sunday evening, as we prepared to go to the evening service, something began to stir in my heart. It was troubling. I really thought that someone in my family was hurt or in trouble. It was just such a heavy burden or weight upon my heart. We arrived at church, and everything progressed as normal, but this feeling wouldn't leave me. We took prayer request as usual because we believed that God heard and answered prayer. I asked the church to pray for my family and myself due to this burden that God had put on my heart. As everyone began to pray and the song leader began to sing, I could stand it no longer, so I went to the altar. I believed then, as I do now, that many of our problems can be solved at an altar of prayer. As I knelt down to pray, I asked God what it was that He was trying to tell me. It wasn't like an audible voice, but it was so powerful. God said, "Preach my word!"

It felt like electricity hit me, and I began to cry uncontrollably. I was going to say *weep*, but it was much uglier than that. As I gained my composure, I asked God again, "What are You trying to tell me?"

Again, I heard, "Preach My word."

Again there was electricity and crying.

The third time I asked, "What is it that You are trying to tell me?"

"Preach My word!"

Power flowed through me, and I surrendered and said, "I will."

I didn't say anything the rest of that service, but as we got in my old truck, I told my wife that I had something to tell her. Before I could say anything, she said, "God has called you to preach, hasn't He?"

More tears flowed.

I said, "I need to talk to Bro. Burcham."

We arrived at the Burchams' house and rang the doorbell. Bro. Burcham answered the door and I said, "I need to talk to you."

He looked at me and said, "God has called you to preach, hasn't He?"

Even more tears went down my eyes.

That calling has kept me going in the ministry ever since. There was a time I doubted my calling and even my salvation, but that calling wouldn't let me stop. As stated in a previous chapter, I have been tempted to stray to my opinions and thoughts, but those don't produce lasting fruit. When you or I preach the Word of God, we have this confidence that it will perform what it says.

> Preach the word; be instant in season, out of season; reprove, rebuke, exhort with all longsuffering and doctrine. (2 Timothy 4:2 KJV)

Personal experience or thoughts: _______________________

____

____

____

____

____

____

____

____

CHAPTER 8

THE PULPIT SHOULD NOT DRIVE YOU TO THE MESSAGE, THE MESSAGE SHOULD DRIVE YOU TO THE PULPIT

This is one of those that was brought to me at exactly the right time, as many of these were.

This usually applies to us after we have been in the ministry for some time. We have honed our skills at sermon preparation or have found a good website with sermon ideas.

The problem is that we are just filling space and doing our duty. We realize that we have to have something for Sunday, so we grab an idea off of the World Wide Web or microwave one we have preached before. I'm not saying you can only preach a sermon once and then throw it away, but you want God to direct you and not your lack of desire. I also realize that every Sunday probably isn't going to be a pew-jumping, aisle-running, devil-slapping message. Whether it is a pastoral (straighten up) sermon or a speak-to-your-mountain sermon, you want to go to the pulpit knowing that you have heard from God, and you have a message to deliver and not just a sermon.

I heard a preacher say once, "We have too many dead preachers preaching dead sermons to a dead congregation."

I am confident that if we will apply ourselves to prayer and study and feed ourselves spiritually, the Holy Spirit will give us fresh bread to deliver to our congregations.

Death and life are in the power of the tongue; speak life.

> If I say, "I will not mention him, or speak any more in his name," there is in my heart as it were a burning fire shut up in my bones, and I am weary with holding it in, and I cannot. (Jeremiah 20:9 ESV)

Oh, that the message will be like a fire shut up in your bones. You can't keep it quiet.

Personal experience or thoughts: ＿＿＿＿＿＿＿＿＿

CHAPTER 9

YOU GET OUT OF A SERMON WHAT YOU PUT INTO IT

Seek for the message, prepare the message, and deliver the message. You cannot expect great results with little effort. Sometimes God will work in spite of us, but you need to prepare. One preacher said, "I preach by the letter, I open up, and let er' fly!" That's funny but a bit frightening also. I have heard a few of those. The message is usually full of clichés, a few stories, and a peppering of amens and well glories. I think of the old man who was asked about a fiery preacher that followed that style of preaching. He said, "There's a lot of thunder but not much rain."

> Study to shew thyself approved unto God, a workman that needeth not to be ashamed, rightly dividing the word of truth. (2 Timothy 2:15 KJV)

Prepare your heart, mind, and spirit. Dig into the Word of God. Don't wait on an invitation to preach before you start studying and reading the Bible. With the resources that are available today, there is no excuse to preach shallow. We tell our people, "You need to get on the meat," but we are not skilled in preparing a good steak.

Everyone's schedules are different. I used to work a forty-hour job and pastor a church with three services. I'm sure that all my sermons weren't barn burners, but I put effort and time into each of them. I get frustrated with preachers that need a two-week notice to preach. Maybe they are getting really prepared. The point I want to make is this: you may have to turn all your screens off and lock yourself in a room for a couple of hours, but take some time to prepare. You really do get out of a sermon or lesson what you put into it.

Personal experience or thoughts: _______________________

____

____

____

____

____

____

____

____

CHAPTER 10

If You Want to Preach a Message with Anointing, You Must Preach an Anointed Message

This is also something I learned early in the ministry. Unfortunately, for some of the congregations I ministered to, not early enough.

I first came to this conclusion after preaching a powerful message with great results. Confusing, isn't it? I assumed that it worked so well the first time, that I would get the same results the next time. When my next opportunity came to preach again, I pulled out the notes, and with much confidence and very little spiritual preparation, I took the pulpit. I said the same things, made the same points, and waited for the same response. Nothing happened; I mean nothing. After I recovered from my bruised ego, here is what I learned.

Even though I had prayed for and received the thought for the message, and it was scripturally sound, it wasn't the message of the hour. The second congregation needed a message from God for them. Now I am not saying that you cannot preach a message more than once, but you need to seek God for His direction and timing. There are many sermon books available, and these are fine to receive thoughts or inspiration from, but you need to spend time in prayer and study, to receive the right message, for the right time, to minister to the right congregation.

I am convinced that, if you have spent the time to receive direction from the Holy Ghost and have the message of the hour, the anointing will be there.

I have heard of young preachers resigning their pastorate after six months because they ran out of things to preach on. This and coming to the place where you rely on books, the internet, or other people's sermons, are usually the result of a lack of prayer and study.

Every preacher has experienced that dreaded Saturday night sermon block. If your well has run dry, dig a little deeper and refill. You may need to be like Isaac and dig the wells again that have been polluted and filled in. Read good inspirational books, listen to some good sermon tapes, even take some time away and attend another church or minister's retreat. If nothing else, call someone to come and preach to you. Notice I said "to you" and not "for you." Get someone who will preach the message of the hour to you.

If the service is dead or dry, it is either the fact that the congregation has not come prepared or the preacher hasn't. Most of the time, I have found it is the latter. We have been called to feed the flock. I grew up in the country, in a time or at least in a house, where there was no microwave oven. As much as things have improved, I have yet to eat a microwave meal that tasted as good as a home-cooked meal. When I would walk into the house, and the aroma of fresh baked bread and the seasonings would welcome me home, I knew something good was coming. It wasn't just the flavors, but knowing the time and love that was involved in the preparation, meant something too. Okay, the flavor was the best! The point is this, we have too many preachers grabbing a sermon out of a file or a book, popping it into the spiritual microwave, and expecting the same results as the one who has prayed, studied, and sought the face of God for the right message for that time. We want oven-baked anointing with Pop-Tarts effort.

I once visited a fellow pastor who pastored a sister church in our town. He was in his study finishing the notes on his upcoming sermon. I asked him if he was finished, and he replied, "Everything but bathing it in prayer." It took me a while to understand what he was saying. I realize now that we must saturate the message with prayer for the Holy Spirit to anoint it.

Preach an anointed message, and you will preach a message with anointing.

> But what saith it? The word is nigh thee, *even* in thy mouth, and in thy heart: that is, the word of faith, which we preach. (Romans 10:8 KJV)

Personal experience or thoughts: _______________________

____

____

____

____

____

____

____

____

CHAPTER 11

IF YOU WANT THE POWER, YOU MUST PAY THE PRICE

This is one of those that I have to remind myself of often. We want to preach and minister with power. Sometimes it seems like the fire is burning and the power is flowing, while at other times, it feels like the coals are smoldering and the battery is dead. What was the difference? The people weren't receiving? The music wasn't right? The preliminaries were off? Maybe, but I have found in my life that, more times than not, it's me. The disciples came to Jesus and asked Him the question about why they couldn't cast a demon out of a boy. Jesus told them, "This kind only comes out through prayer and fasting." I'm pretty good at praying fast, but I don't think that is what Jesus meant. It is the prayer and fasting, the seeking God, the worship in spirit and truth, the sowing to the spirit, before you face the devil.

Where does the power come from? From connecting to the Vine (Jesus Christ) and being filled with the Holy Spirit.

> But ye shall receive power, after that the Holy Ghost is come upon you: and ye shall be witnesses unto me both in Jerusalem, and in all Judaea, and in Samaria, and unto the uttermost part of the earth. (Acts 1:8 KJV)

> Now when they saw the boldness of Peter and John, and perceived that they were unlearned

and ignorant men, they marvelled; and they took knowledge of them, that they had been with Jesus. (Acts 4:13 KJV)

Just like our beloved cell phones, we must plug in to God to receive the power that we need to walk in His overcoming power. God is not stingy with His power. He wants to see His children overcome and live the abundant life.

Much of what we see on the news and that's happening in our society is spiritual. This is the Church's time to rise up and shine! We must make the time to connect to the source of power, the Holy Spirit of God. We must spend time with Jesus. You cannot expect full-time benefits with part-time efforts.

Personal experience or thoughts: _________________________

____

____

____

____

____

____

____

CHAPTER 12

IF YOU'RE NOT CERTAIN, DON'T SAY IT

When is the baby due? I'm not pregnant! Being a very outgoing person who likes to converse with people around me, I have learned this lesson the hard way. I would like to say it only took once. If she isn't wearing a "Baby on Board" or a "Coming Soon" maternity top, talk about the weather.

In this age of great knowledge and technology, it is amazing how much false information we are fed. I saw a picture of Abraham Lincoln making a post on social media, so it must be true.

Sometimes, we preachers, in search of a good illustration, will embellish a story, quote someone, or completely fabricate something to make a point. I have been known to use an unrelated scripture as a jumping-off spot to preach on a topic that I wanted to preach on. Truthfully, that message was more opinion than biblical truth. I do want to clarify that this was very early in my ministry when I had more zeal than wisdom.

I have also repeated illustrations that I had heard and believed were true, only to find out later that even though it was a great story, it wasn't true. That's a little embarrassing, but if you are quick-minded enough, you just explain it was a parable and not a real-life experience.

The real point of this proverb is that if you don't know without a doubt it is true or really in the Bible, don't say it. Aunt Gertrude was a wonderful church lady, but just because she used *thee* and *thou* and ended all her words with a *th* on the end doesn't mean they were or are in the Bible. If you find yourself preaching and repeating terms like "I think" or "I believe" or "I feel," you need to take the time to check the facts.

If a dear saint comes to share a prayer need with you about someone else in the church (gossip), get the facts before you set up a counseling session.

> Sanctify them through thy truth: thy word is truth. (John 17:17 KJV)

Remember, the truth will make you free.

Personal experience or thoughts: _______________

____

____

____

____

____

____

____

____

CHAPTER 13

EVEN A FOOL SEEMS WISE IF HE KEEPS HIS MOUTH SHUT

This is actually found in the book of Proverbs and is very true:

> Even a fool, when he holdeth his peace, is counted wise: *and* he that shutteth his lips *is esteemed* a man of understanding. (Proverbs 17:28 KJV)

If you know me personally, then you know that I have a comment on almost everything others say. In my mind, I think my remarks are witty and hilarious. Sometimes they are funny, but sometimes, they are at the wrong time. At other times, I'm sure that people are just oversensitive. Okay, so I am learning that everything that pops into my head isn't a word from God, and it doesn't need to be said.

A merry heart does good like a medicine, but jesting at the wrong time is like a fly in the ointment. I do see the humor in many things, but my people need to know that their pastor or minister can be serious and be genuinely concerned about their needs. I used to feel like I had to have the answer for every question. I would try to bluff my way through with some spiritual cliché (i.e., that is a great question and I could give you the answer, but I feel like God would have you seek Him for the revelation.)

I have come to the place that I can say, "I don't know, but we both can dig into that and see what we come up with." It doesn't hurt to be a little transparent with your congregation.

In some situations, it's better to just be quiet and observe.

Another proverb that was told me was, "It is better to be quiet and let people think you are a fool, then to open your mouth and remove all doubt."

Personal experience or thoughts: ________________________

____

____

____

____

____

____

____

____

CHAPTER 14

IT DOESN'T HAVE TO BE ETERNAL TO BE IMMORTAL

> But when ye pray, use not vain repetitions, as the
> heathen *do*: for they think that they shall be heard
> for their much speaking. (Matthew 6:7 KJV)

I read that the Pharisees would stand on the street corners and pray sometimes for three hours. I can't imagine what their sermon would be like!

This may be what you are thinking about this book. What does this mean? Your messages or lessons don't have to last for eternity to impact eternity. I have heard some great preachers who preach for an hour and keep you on the edge of your seat because of the anointing. I have heard other preachers preach for an hour and keep you on the edge of your seat in anticipation of the ending.

There are many sayings that communicate the same thing shared among preachers, mostly older ministers who have great wisdom and experience. From the days of hard wooden benches with straight backs, the mind can only receive what the seat can endure. Stand up, and they will see you. Speak up, and they will hear you. Shut up, and they will love you. One of my favorites in the form of a beatitude, "Blessed are the short winded for they shall be called back."

I heard a story of a young country preacher who was concerned about his evening service because a bad snowstorm had blown in.

Since he lived by the church, he went over, started a fire in the old potbellied stove, and waited to see if any of his parishioners would show up. One old farmer came in with a blast of cold air and snow following him through the door. The pastor said, "Well, Bill, it looks like it's just you and me. What do you think we should do?"

Bill said, "Pastor, if I go out to feed hay to my cows and only one shows up, I still feed the one." So the pastor went to the pulpit, took his text, and for the next forty-five minutes, he preached like a house on fire! When he finished, he went back to Bill, shook his hand, and thanked him for coming out. The pastor asked the old farmer what he thought of the message, and Bill spoke with that country drawl, "Preacher, if I go out to feed hay to my cows and only one cow shows up, I don't feed it the whole truckload of hay."

You don't have to preach everything you know when you get an opportunity. Who knows? They may ask you to come back some time. I have come to the end of a message when preaching and realize I had missed a point that I was going to make. I would go back to make that point, and it would not have the effect I had hoped. I have now come to the belief that the Holy Spirit caused me to miss it the first time, and therefore, it should be left out.

When you see that you are losing the congregation, wrap it up.

Personal experience or thoughts: ________________________

____

____

____

____

____

____

____

____

CHAPTER 15

THERE IS AT LEAST ONE LESS GREAT PREACHER THAN YOU THINK

Pride *goeth* before destruction, and a haughty spirit before a fall.

—Proverbs 16:18 (KJV)

There was a preacher that had just pulled out of the church parking lot after a Sunday morning service. He was feeling especially proud of his sermon and his delivery that morning. In desperate need of having his ego confirmed, he said to his wife, "There are a lot of great preachers aren't there?"

His wife, without even looking up, said, "One less than you think."

Remember you are what you are because of Jesus Christ. Pride sets you up for a fall, but humility gives you space to be exalted. Don't allow people's praises go to your head; more on that later.

Jesus was one of the humblest and yet unarguably the most powerful being to walk on this planet. Help us, Lord, to be more like Jesus.

I have come to realize that every time I begin to think I'm all that and a bag of chips, God sends someone by to get me back on the ground.

Blessed *are* the meek: for they shall inherit the earth. (Matthew 5:5 KJV)

Personal experience or thoughts: ______________

____

____

____

____

____

____

____

____

____

CHAPTER 16

BEWARE OF THE VULTURES

This chapter was originally called "Beware of the Buzzards," but we have some good friends with the last name Buzzard, derived from a French name. I thought it would be better to change it.

There are always vultures circling around, especially if things are going well in your church. They are a lot like Absalom, David's son. In the Bible, it tells us of how Absalom began to encourage the people to look to him for guidance. He was trying to get a following so that he could take the kingdom from David.

> And Absalom rose up early, and stood beside the way of the gate: and it was *so*, that when any man that had a controversy came to the king for judgment, then Absalom called unto him, and said, Of what city *art* thou? And he said, Thy servant *is* of one of the tribes of Israel. And Absalom said unto him, See, thy matters *are* good and right; but *there is* no man *deputed* of the king to hear thee. Absalom said moreover, Oh that I were made judge in the land, that every man which hath any suit or cause might come unto me, and I would do him justice! And it was *so*, that when any man came nigh *to him* to do him obeisance, he put forth his hand, and took him, and kissed him. And on this manner did Absalom

to all Israel that came to the king for judgment:
so Absalom stole the hearts of the men of Israel.
(2 Samuel 15:2–6 KJV; emphasis mine)

This is where the gift of discernment is important. Is it my own insecurity, or is it a vulture trying to pick off the weaker members?

I have had ministers in my churches that would take over a service or would seem to be at the hospital or house of the sick when I arrived. I tried to convince myself that they were just caring and concerned, but something in my spirit didn't feel right. Then I began to get reports of them calling members of the church, telling them that I wasn't pastoring like I should and began to attack my character. They decided to start their own church and took families with them.

On a lighter side, one evening, we had a young man whom I had never met attend our service. As is our custom at times, we had a testimony service, a time where anyone in the congregation can stand and give (hopefully) a positive word of what God had done or was doing in their life. This young man, who was sitting on the back pew, stood up and began sharing. It wasn't long before he was in full preaching mode and had made his way to the front of the sanctuary. I had firmly gripped the pulpit because I knew that if he got behind the pulpit, I might lose the whole service. He looked back at me and said, "Can I have two more minutes?" He wasn't saying anything bad or trying to lead people astray; he was just excited about Jesus and salvation. I looked at my watch and said, "Go!" He took off proclaiming his love for the Lord and his joy at being set free from his sins. He sat down, and I said, "You have twenty seconds left." He jumped up and began talking again. When the twenty seconds were up, I said, "Time!" He sat down, and the service went on. He wasn't there to cause trouble or to lead people away from the truth. I could tell that from his spirit and the Holy Spirit.

I am a very nonconfrontational person, but I have had meetings with those who were bringing confusion and division into the church. Not only do you feed the flock, but at times you must protect the flock.

Personal experience or thoughts: _______________________

____

____

____

____

____

____

____

____

CHAPTER 17

SOMETIMES YOU ARE CALLED JUST TO START SOMETHING

A pioneering spirit, this is what I call it—that drive and desire to do and build for the kingdom of God.

At the end of WWII, many of those who served their country came back and began to serve God. I don't know if their experiences in the war influenced their gratitude toward God, but I know several of the older preachers that I knew as a young Christian had served in the military, some in WWII and some in Korea. Maybe it was just the greatest generation, but they had a pioneering spirit. They went out and began to preach with little or no assistance from any organization other than prayer and fellowship. They would seek God for direction, and when they had heard from God, they packed up the family and went. Many of us are still experiencing the benefits of their faithfulness.

I'm not saying that there may be improved ways of planting a church, but I am saying that, in my opinion, we have lost that "honey, pack the car and the kids, we are going to build a church" spirit. What does it pay? How many does it run? What kind of package do they offer?

Statistics tells us that there are thousands of churches closing each year, and that breaks my heart.

Some of the churches that have been planted didn't make it, but others thrived. If we don't try, we will never know. I have seen church plants that seemed to fail, but the remaining members connected with another congregation, and both were blessed.

Some are definitely called to receive the baton and run with it, but somebody has to start the race.

Whether it is a church plant, a Bible study, a neighborhood fellowship, or a church cleaning crew, somebody has to light the match.

Despise not small beginnings. Remember we walk by faith.

> Do not despise these small beginnings, for the LORD rejoices to see the work begin, to see the plumb line in Zerubbabel's hand. (The seven lamps represent the eyes of the LORD that search all around the world). (Zechariah 4:10 NLT)

Yes, by all means, count the cost. Plan the work, and work the plan. Work to prepare yourself for the challenge before you. Faith is working without seeing exactly how it will end.

We started the church we now pastor from almost nothing, but we really felt God leading us. As of the writing of this book, we have been here for twenty-two years. We have seen many changes and met many new people, and we still do not know exactly what all God has planned for us, but we rest assured that He has a plan. If God tarries, someone else will pick up the baton here and continue this ministry.

So just start something.

Personal experience or thoughts: _______________________

____

____

____

____

____

____

____

____

Chapter 18

Never See Your People as a Paycheck

This not only a bad place to be as a minister, but it may very well be a sign of a couple of things.

When you begin to stress when the crowd is low because you're worried about how you are going to make your car payment, you may be seeing your church as a paycheck. I understand that we who preach the gospel, live off the gospel, but our hearts must be for the establishment of the body of Christ.

It can be a sign of a spiritual deficiency in your own life. You are caught in the routine, and it has become your job and not your passion. Go to God in prayer, and ask Him to search your heart and reveal it to you. He will. Then pray it through. That is an old-time phrase that means to pray until you get a breakthrough. Speak to a mature minister that you have confidence in. He has probably been where you are at.

The other thing it might be a sign of is that God has released you from that position and is trying to move you to another area of ministry. Even we preachers, we spiritual giants, get comfortable with things. The danger of becoming too comfortable is that we have lost the passion and burden for the people and just enjoy the comfort of the position.

Your people are eternal beings in which God has put you in their lives to lead and help them in their spiritual walk.

Don't allow their giving to determine which ones get the most attention.

> My brethren, have not the faith of our Lord Jesus
> Christ, *the Lord* of glory, with respect of persons.
> (James 2:1 KJV)

A sign I seen at a church once read, "This ministry is not coin operated. Make sure it isn't."

Personal experience or thoughts: _______________________

____

____

____

____

____

____

____

____

CHAPTER 19

DON'T MAJOR ON THE MINORS

This is a sign of a Pharisee spirit. Jesus said that they would strain a gnat and swallow a camel. Before anyone writes me and tells me it is physically impossible to swallow a camel whole, let me remind you it was a word picture, just an illustration or an allegory to make a point about how the Pharisees would be critical of the smallest offence but accept and allow major sins.

It is very easy to begin to major on the minors, to make mountains out of molehills. Again, this is a spiritual condition. Either you are extremely paranoid that everyone is going to miss heaven because they jaywalked, or you feel like it exalts you to point out everyone else's faults.

I was that person. I saw everything with a critical eye. I remember listening to our local Christian radio station. It was even Southern gospel, none of that worldly contemporary stuff (that's a joke). I was shocked one day when I heard that a beauty supply store was one of their sponsors. Yes, you heard right, a makeup supplier! The Jezebel store! I had been told that makeup was evil. I will say that makeup may be deceptive, and there have been fellows who have woken up in the morning and feel like some stranger has slipped into his house!

Sorry, I was trying to be funny, but honestly, I looked at everything with a critical eye, thinking that so much was sinful. I felt like the radio station was compromising their Christian testimony.

If that is a real conviction that you have, stick to it. More power to you. If it's something you heard with no scriptural backing or just a preference, leave it alone. Remember, a conviction is something you would die for.

Major on the important things like salvation, the truth of God's Word, and the fullness of the Spirit. I have found that, if we can get people connected to God, He will do the rest. Everyone doesn't grow at the same rate, and everyone is not the same age spiritually. Give the Holy Spirit room to work.

We had a young lady who was gloriously saved and set free from a life of addiction! She had no church background at all (which is wonderful). She was hungry for and growing in the Lord. One day, "a very concerned" member (sarcasm intended) messaged me that the new convert had been seen at a bar with a beer in her hand. I always wondered how the member had seen her at the bar. Anyway, I was instructed that I should promptly deal with this indiscretion. I committed it to prayer and trusted the Holy Spirit to do what He does. We received a call a few days later from the new convert. She said, "The other night, I was invited to go out with some old friends to the bar, and I went. I was given a beer, I took one sip, and it just didn't taste right. I looked around me, and I felt something inside telling me that this isn't the place I need to be." That was years ago, and now she is still serving God and even speaking at times. God is good!

> Or how can you say to your brother, "Let me take the speck out of your eye," when there is a log in your own eye? You hypocrite, first take the log out of your own eye, and then you will see clearly to take the speck out of your brother's eye. (Matthew 7:4–5 ESV)

I am convinced that we will find that grace is much more amazing than we think.

Personal experience or thoughts: ___________________________

____

____

____

____

____

____

____

____

ADD A LITTLE HUMOR, DON'T TAKE YOURSELF SO SERIOUSLY

Mary Poppins sang, "Just a spoonful of sugar helps the medicine go down." I referred to using humor in a previous chapter. Timing really is everything, not your comedic timing, even though that is very important but *when* you try to be funny.

I have a tendency to see humor in many things. I think it is a coping mechanism I learned early in life due to some very traumatic events. Some people have told me, and I quote, "You just aren't right in the head."

To which I laugh and say, "Well, what would the fun be in that?" I have found that through the use of humor, people will lower their guard and be more open to receive the serious stuff.

I once had a cortisone shot in my shoulder due to some intense pain I was having (in my shoulder). I felt as though I needed to clear that up for some of you readers. The nurse prepped me by rubbing the disinfectant on the back of my shoulder. The doctor instructed me to hug myself. That was nice, and I needed a hug to calm me down. The doctor then proceeded to shove a 1/4-in-diameter twelve-inch-long spear that he called a needle into my shoulder. He pushed and worked it around inside my shoulder until it almost poked out the front of my body (some of that may have been a slight exaggeration). After he was done, he said, "If it gets to hurting like that again, come back, and we will give you another shot." I thought to myself (which seems to be the only way I can think), *It will never hurt that bad again.*

Fast-forward several years, and now my knee is causing me great pain, literally unbearable. I was taking all the over-the-counter pain meds I could take safely without destroying my kidneys or my liver. I knew that I would probably have to get a shot in my knee. I base that on the fact that the orthopedic doctor told me that the next time my knee caused me troubles, I would need to get a shot of cortisone in it. I dreaded it and put it off until I could stand it no longer.

I went to the ortho doctor with fear and in trepidation. Again, the nurse cleaned the spot of the injection. The doctor came in (different doctor) and told me that I would feel a very cold spray on the side of my knee. I closed my eyes and began to fast and pray immediately. I felt the very cold spray, and as I was about to be caught up into the third heaven, I heard the doctor say, "Okay, that should last you a few months, but if it starts giving you trouble, feel free to call me."

You are probably thinking, what does that story have to do with using humor? Humor is like that spray that softens the point of the medicine that is needed. Plus, I just love to tell stories.

> A merry heart doeth good *like* a medicine: but a broken spirit drieth the bones. (Proverbs 17:22 KJV)

There is a time to laugh, and there is a time to cry. I enjoy the laughter more. The world hears negative and depressive news all the time. Give them something to smile about.

Remember, a word spoken at the right time is a powerful thing. Don't take yourself too seriously.

Personal experience or thoughts: _______________________

____

____

____

____

____

____

____

____

CHAPTER 21

PEOPLE NEED TO KNOW HOW MUCH YOU CARE BEFORE THEY CARE HOW MUCH YOU KNOW

I genuinely like people. When I go places with my grown children, I meet people I know all the time. They have asked me many times, "Dad, do you know everyone?"

My answer has become, "Not yet!"

The old joke between preachers is, "I love the ministry—I just don't like people."

Let me say this as clearly as I can, and I am not being humorous. If you don't like people, get saved. If that doesn't change your heart, get out of the ministry.

> If a man say, I love God, and hateth his brother,
> he is a liar: for he that loveth not his brother
> whom he hath seen, how can he love God whom
> he hath not seen? (1 John 4:20 KJV)

Jesus loved people. Even the ones that irritated Him, He loved. He especially loved the hurting, lost sinners.

Once, I had the privilege to preach a youth camp in Arkansas. My wife and I was in our element. We love the youth, and they seemed to tolerate us. Every day we would get up early, head to the campground, and hang out with the kids.

The camp director came to me later in the week, and he said, "I want to thank you for spending time with the campers."

I was shocked because I thought that is what camp speakers do. He told me that we were the first speakers that he had speak at his camps that came to hang out with the kids. He said, "Most only show up when it's time to speak."

That bothered me greatly.

It's not about my ministry; it's about me ministering. Much of that is done outside of the pulpit. Jesus was all about relationships. Why did Jesus weep at the grave of Lazarus? Maybe because of their doubt, but I am convinced he wept because Mary and Martha were hurting and weeping. I believe He felt the pain of Lazarus having to suffer and die.

If you aren't building relationships, you are missing a rewarding part of ministry. If people see you as untouchable, they probably won't be very receptive of your message.

> He that loveth his brother abideth in the light,
> and there is none occasion of stumbling in him.
> (1 John 2:10 KJV)

Personal experience or thoughts: _________________________

____

____

____

____

____

____

____

____

CHAPTER 22

DON'T BE CONCEITED—
NOT EVERYONE IS
TALKING ABOUT YOU

Paranoia—the *Merriam-Webster Dictionary* defines it as a "mental illness characterized by systematized delusions of persecution or grandeur usually without hallucinations."

I have heard that you don't have to be crazy to be a pastor, but it helps.

The second definition better describes what I am talking about—"a tendency on the part of an individual or group toward excessive or irrational suspiciousness and distrustfulness of others."

I have met individuals who are in a life of addiction to drugs, whose lives are controlled by this kind of paranoia. I was talking to a man who I found sleeping on our church steps. As we talked, he pointed out the blinking lights of an airplane and told me they were government agents that had been following him. It is terribly sad to see a person controlled by that kind of fear.

I have been at that place before, minus the drugs. I was pastoring a small church in rural Missouri that had a very domineering board made up of two men. They would call me into a meeting to correct something I had or hadn't done. I became so obsessed with worrying about what they were talking about every time I had seen them together. It seemed they were always together. It really became a paranoia.

One Sunday morning before service, both men and their wives were standing in a group talking. God had sent me an older minister; I believe to help and encourage me. I said to him, "Look at them over there talking about me."

He looked me in the eye and with a wry smile said, "Don't be so conceited. Not everyone talks about you." I laughed out loud (literally) and realized he was right.

Oh, we had our conflicts from time to time, but sometimes, they were just talking about fishing or the weather.

> Which of you by taking thought can add one
> cubit unto his stature? (Matthew 6:27 KJV)

Over and over, Jesus taught, saying, "Take no thought." Don't worry, don't stress. Many pastors drop out of the ministry, and sadly, we are seeing an increase of suicide in the ministry. We are results driven.

"How is your church doing?"

"Oh, we are blessed."

"Who is going to leave?"

"Who is talking and stirring up division?"

"Are the leaders with me?"

"Will I be able to take care of my family?"

The paranoia kept me from seeing *all* the people in my church and their needs. Plus, it sucked the joy out of my church experience and hindered my worship.

I attended the funeral of one of those men years later. As they spoke of his service in the military and in business and his life in general, I was profoundly moved. I openly wept as I thought of how much we could have accomplished together had I not allowed my fear to control my thoughts toward him.

It's not about you or me.

Personal experience or thoughts: ___________________________
____

____

____

____

____

____

____

____

CHAPTER 23

REMEMBER THE JOAB FACTOR

I don't want to contradict the previous chapter or cause you to be paranoid, but you do need to be sensitive to the Spirit. Pray for the gift of discernment.

> Beloved, believe not every spirit, but try the spirits whether they are of God: because many false prophets are gone out into the world. (1 John 4:1 KJV)

We are also told to know those who work with you.

Joab was good with his left hand. He would greet others by grasping their beard with his right hand (which is usually your strong hand), seeming to show vulnerability. While he was greeting them and embracing them as a friend would do, he would reach with his left hand, grasp his knife, and stab them under the fifth rib.

> And Joab said to Amasa, "*Art* thou in health, my brother?" And Joab took Amasa by the beard with the right hand to kiss him. But Amasa took no heed to the sword that *was* in Joab's hand: so he smote him therewith in the fifth *rib*, and shed out his bowels to the ground, and struck him not again; and he died. So Joab and Abishai his

brother pursued after Sheba the son of Bichri. (2
Samuel 20:9–10 KJV)

In the ministry, especially as a pastor, you have to be careful
who you allow to get close to you. It is hard to have a real close
friend in the congregation. It can bring either jealousy from others or
the expectation of preferential treatment. However, we in the ministry do need friends and confidants, maybe another minister whom
you can trust, even across denominational lines. I encourage you to
connect with the local Ministerial Alliance. Yes, we are different in
our doctrine and theology, but we all face very similar situations in
ministry.

The real point of this teaching is that you need to know those
whom you allow to get close to you. Make sure they are loyal and
trustworthy, not someone who is looking for an opportunity to find
something to hurt you with.

Personal experience or thoughts: _______________________

____
____
____
____
____
____
____
____

CHAPTER 24

HE WHO SOUNDS THE TRUMPET THE LOUDEST USUALLY DOES THE LEAST

This, too, is a Pharisee spirit. They stand and pray seemingly forever or tell everyone about how much they pray or read the Bible. They share how much they have given to the missionaries. They just want everyone else to know how much of a blessing they are to the church.

They really think that if everyone in the church were just like them, it would be an awesome church.

They are looking for a stage and not a platform. They are always talking about everything they have done for God. Their testimonies are about how they blessed those around them and nothing about what God has done or is doing—me, me, me all the way.

They never volunteer to help with the work of the church. They are the first ones gone when it's time to clean up after fellowship (that's Christianese for eating). If they do show up for a workday, they are only there to tell stories of when they built an entire church by themselves or to tell you how you are doing it wrong.

It reminds me of a verse in the book of James, "Show me your faith without your works, and I will show you my faith by my works."

> These are spots in your feasts of charity, when they feast with you, feeding themselves without fear: clouds *they are* without water, carried

about of winds; trees whose fruit withereth, without fruit, twice dead, plucked up by the roots. (Jude 1:12 KJV)

Much thunder, no rain.

Personal experience or thoughts: ______________________

____

____

____

____

____

____

____

____

____

CHAPTER 25

THE CLOSER TO GOD YOU ARE, THE LESS YOU HAVE TO TELL PEOPLE HOW CLOSE TO GOD YOU ARE

This is similar to the previous chapter, except it was talking about others, and this one is talking about you. If you are always trying to convince people of your spirituality, there is probably something lacking, maybe it's self-esteem or maybe you are covering up something. I remember a Sunday school class I was teaching in my first pastorate, it was the young adults. One of the students who was probably actually older than me made a statement/question and said, "I'm sure that Pastor Reed knows all about that." Of course I did what most insecure young pastors would do—I lied. I said, "Oh, yes, definitely, it is crazy what is happening in the Middle East."

To which she followed up with, "How do you mean, and what do you think it is?"

I was busted. I admitted that I wasn't very familiar with what she was talking about, but I would make a point of checking it out; I did.

It was kind of like when Jesus instructed His disciples to take the lower seat when invited to a dinner. It's less humbling to be asked to move up instead of down.

I realize, even after thirty-three years, I do not know everything. There is no shame in admitting that unless it is elementary. My study and knowledge have grown, as well as my prayer life and understanding. I don't need to tell you all those things because if I am close to God, you will know without me telling you. Again, to quote an old commercial, "The proof is in the pudding."

> And my speech and my preaching *was* not
> with enticing words of man's wisdom, but
> in demonstration of the Spirit and of power.
> (1 Corinthians 2:4 KJV)

Personal experience or thoughts: _______________________

____

____

____

____

____

____

____

____

Chapter 26

Praises Are Sweet, but Too Many Sweets Are Bad for You

Everyone likes to be appreciated and told they are doing a good job. We can even say that we need that positive feedback. I believe that almost everyone's love language involves affirmation. The danger is when the affirmation turns to flattery.

Our ego can get us into a lot of trouble. We can be drawn into impure and immoral relationships. First, it can cause you to develop favorites. I realize that there will be people in your congregation that you can connect with better, but flattery can cause you to spend all your time and energy with certain individuals. Of course, we all would rather be around people who always talk about how great we are and how we made such a difference in their lives, but having our ego stroked continually can cause us to start believing that we are pretty amazing. We can cross from confidence to conceit very easily. Pride goes before destruction.

> Woe unto you, when all men shall speak well of
> you! for so did their fathers to the false prophets.
> (Luke 6:26 KJV)

Remember, this ministry is about Jesus and not about you.

Secondly, flattery can lead us into immoral relationships with the opposite sex and sometimes with the same. Be cautious not to allow yourself to be alone with the opposite sex unless it is your spouse. If I have a girl or woman that wants counseling, I try to direct her to my wife or another mature, godly woman. If she insists that she needs to talk to me, she will meet with my wife and I.

As a young pastor, I worked at a secular job. One day, this young woman came up to me and began to share that she and her husband were having troubles. Then came the flattery: "I know that you are a minister, and I have seen you here at work. You are so easy to talk to, and I need some spiritual direction." That was more compelling than if she would have said, "You're a good-looking man." Why yes, I am a pastor and a spiritual giant. Allow me to bring revelation and solve all your problems.

Thankfully, God brought revelation to me through my wife. She came walking through the door of the store I was working in with our three children in tow. I was sitting in the break area with the troubled young woman. Suddenly, I could see clearly!

Ministers need to know that they are appreciated and that they are making a difference, but when someone seems to really be heaping on the sugar, back away.

This can also be with any member or family in your congregation. When the compliment turns to flattery, special treatment can be expected by the flatterer. Listen to the Holy Spirit and your spouse.

Personal experience or thoughts: _______________________

____

____

____

____

____

____

____

____

CHAPTER 27

WHEN SOMEONE TELLS YOU THAT GOD LED THEM TO YOUR CHURCH, REST ASSURED, HE WILL LEAD THEM SOMEWHERE ELSE SOON

This sounds like a statement of a bitter pastor. Understand this, God will lead people your way, and they will be a great blessing to you. Some come for a season, some come for a reason, and some are just passing through.

Allow me to talk about that statement for a moment. Some will come by for a season. God will bring them by to serve or bring the ministry to a certain level. Maybe it is a season that they are going through in which they need your ministry to bring them to a certain level or healing.

Some come for a reason. God has brought people to us that were hurting, wounded, or just burned out. They were with us for the purpose to rest and recover. They needed us to pour into them and help them prepare to get back into the battle. I love ministering to the ministry.

Some are just passing through, searching for something, and trying to find a place where they fit.

None of these make a proclamation, when they first come in, that God sent them. They may at a latter time testify that God brought them to you. Thank God for the ones He sends in that find Jesus in their lives who become planted and stay with you. In this day and time, it is a great blessing to hear someone say, "This is my church," and mean it.

Those who walk through your front door or attend their first service and make a proclamation that the spirit has led them to your ministry will probably be led by the same spirit soon. Notice I used the lowercase *s* on the word *spirit*. It is not the Holy Spirit that is leading them but their own spirit. Most will notify you right away that God has called them to preach, or teach, or sing, or prophesy, or something else, and if you are the man of God that they think you are, you will use them immediately. Amazingly, I have never had anyone come in and proclaim, "I am called to the cleaning ministry." They are looking for a stage and not a platform. They aren't about building the kingdom of God; they are about building a fanbase.

If you don't use them or allow them to exercise their gifts immediately, they will be led elsewhere.

> That we *henceforth* be no more children, tossed to and fro, and carried about with every wind of doctrine, by the sleight of men, *and* cunning craftiness, whereby they lie in wait to deceive. (Ephesians 4:14 KJV)

Personal experience or thoughts: __________________

____

____

____

____

____

____

____

CHAPTER 28

WHEN IN DOUBT, DO WITHOUT

As a young Christian, I was always asking my pastor questions about doing the right thing. I had very little church background, and I sure didn't want to mess up this amazing thing that God had done in my life. I wanted to live an overcoming and victorious life. Also, I didn't realize that being a Christian was more than just following rules. So when I asked him for the umpteenth time, "Is this okay?"

He told me this, "When in doubt, do without."

Obviously, he encouraged me to search the Scriptures for myself to find the truth and direction of God, but as a young believer, this really was good advice. I didn't miss anything that drastically changed my life, but I did avoid some pitfalls. I have seen those who continue to hang out with the same crowd or get involved in things that a young Christian just isn't strong enough for, only to be pulled back into the world. Even though we are New Testament believers, there are still warnings and commands of, "Don't go there, and don't do that." The lust of the flesh, the lust of the eyes, and the pride of life exist.

I have often said in my preaching, "If you are trying to see how close to the world you can get and still be saved or pleasing to God, you have already gone too far." We should see how close to God we can get and still be on this planet.

Better *is* a little with righteousness than great revenues without right. (Proverbs 16:8 KJV)

There are some gray areas in our walk with God. There are many voices and opinions vying for your attention. Do this. Don't do this. There are some things that aren't spelled out for us. We have to seek God and allow the Holy Spirit to guide us. Maybe that doubt is the Holy Spirit, so the safe thing to do is this: when in doubt, do without.

Personal experience or thoughts: ________________________

____

____

____

____

____

____

____

____

Chapter 29

Be a Person after God's Own Heart, and Be a Person after the Heart of God

> And when he had removed him, he raised up unto them David to be their king; to whom also he gave testimony, and said, I have found David the son of Jesse, a man after mine own heart, which shall fulfil all my will. (Acts 13:22 KJV)

What a testimony! To be a person with a heart like God's, we know that David was quick to repent when confronted with his sin by Nathan, the prophet. He was a man who believed in, loved, and executed justice. He was a man who loved to worship in the presence of God.

I have always read this a little differently than saying, "David's heart was like the heart of God." I believe that is true, but I read it as, "David was after the heart of God." As I said, David was what I call a "praiser." I know that isn't a word because I am a reader and because my spell check has it underlined in red but he was! He would dance at the drop of a hat or, more literally, at the drop of his royal robes. He said things like, "I was glad when they said unto me, let us go into the house of the Lord today."

> One *thing* have I desired of the LORD, that will I seek after; that I may dwell in the house of the LORD all

the days of my life, to behold the beauty of the Lord,
and to enquire in his temple. (Psalm 27:4 KJV)

Through praise and worship of God, attending church, prayer, and study of the Bible and good Christian authors, we draw closer to God's heart. Through loving, serving, and sharing the good news of Jesus Christ to people, we capture the heart of God.

We know if we know Jesus and walk in truth and obedience in holiness and righteousness, God's blessings will chase us down and overtake us.

And all these blessings shall come on thee, and
overtake thee, if thou shalt hearken unto the voice
of the Lord thy God. (Deuteronomy 28:2 KJV)

We all love and desire the blessings of God, but how hard are we chasing after the heart of God? I want to bless God! I want my heart to be a reflection of God's heart, but I also want to pursue and capture God's heart, to experience that beautiful relationship of communion with God. I remember when our first child was born. I loved my wife, and I loved my family and friends, but when I laid eyes on that little baby girl, she had my heart. I want God's heart in that way. I will continue to pursue it all my days. I am a man after God's heart.

Bless the Lord, O my soul: and all that is within
me, *bless* his holy name. (Psalm 103:1 KJV)

Personal experience or thoughts: _______________________
____
____
____
____
____
____
____
____

CHAPTER 30

SEEK PURPOSE NOT POSITION

*Not with eyeservice, as menpleasers; but as the servants
of Christ, doing the will of God from the heart.*

—Ephesians 6:6 (KJV)

It is challenging when you move from the secular work force into the ministry. In the world, success is based upon promotion. The more titles, or degrees, or positions, or boards you sit on, the more successful you are. We think the natural process of time and achievement leads us upward.

The very word *ministry* means to serve. Even though there is honor, and we should honor men and women ordained of God for ministry, the path to success might been seen as a downward move. Ministry has taught me minor electronics, sanitation, and plumbing, as well as bus driving, and snow removal. I have stood in the pulpit and preached to hundreds, and I have sat at a kitchen table and cried with one.

If position is what you seek, you will find that not only is it lonely at the top, but it is empty. We are called to build God's kingdom and not our own. That doesn't mean that God can't or won't exalt you, but the Bible says that He does that for the humble. If your desire is riches and stuff, ministry may not be for you.

> Jesus said unto him, If thou wilt be perfect, go *and* sell that thou hast, and give to the poor, and thou shalt have treasure in heaven: and come *and* follow me. But when the young man heard that saying, he went away sorrowful: for he had great possessions. (Matthew 19:21–22 KJV)

Again, I'm not saying that you can't be physically and materially blessed, I am saying you must keep your priorities straight.

> No one can serve two masters, for either he will hate the one and love the other, or he will be devoted to the one and despise the other. You cannot serve God and money. (Matthew 6:24 ESV)

It's not wrong to have money as long as the money does not have you. If you are seeking purpose, you will find a truly successful life. As you see lives changed and the joy of the Lord on the faces of those you serve, you realize that you are truly rich. At the time of this writing, I have been in pastoral ministry for thirty-five years. I am still blessed and excited to see God work through me to touch lives. I don't live in a big house or have a large bank account, but I am extremely rich. My four children and their spouses are active in ministry with my beautiful wife and I. I have found my purpose in this life, which has led me to different positions. It's the purpose that makes the difference. Positions eventually go to someone else; purpose lasts a lifetime.

> I thank Christ Jesus our Lord, who has given me strength to do his work. He considered me trustworthy and appointed me to serve him. (1 Timothy 1:12 NLT)

Thank You, Lord, for purpose.

Personal experience or thoughts: _______________________

____

____

____

____

____

____

____

____

CHAPTER 31

WHEN YOU FEEL LIKE QUITTING, AND YOU WILL, DON'T

You have made it to the last chapter! This chapter is a personal message from me to you.

> But ye, brethren, be not weary in well doing. (2 Thessalonians 3:13 KJV)

In the previous chapter, I was thanking God for calling me into the ministry, and I meant it. But to say it has always been easy and that there haven't been times that I have questioned everything from my calling to my salvation and even the existence of God Himself would be a lie. There have been times that all those were true. There were times that I told God that I would just connect myself to a local church and help the pastor in any way he needed. Some would call that God's permissive will, that is a spiritual terminology for *justifiable disobedience*. Of course, neither of those are going to work with God. Partial obedience is still disobedience. I'm not trying to move into legalism, I'm just letting you know that God won't let you get away with it. The calling comes with conviction. I once left a pastorate with that very intention. I hadn't set in my home church for three weeks when the fire and the calling began to pull at my heart again.

What causes us to get to the place that we want to hang up our tie (I'm a little old-school) and walk away?

> Men's hearts failing them for fear, and for look-
> ing after those things which are coming on the
> earth: for the powers of heaven shall be shaken.
> (Luke 21:26 KJV)

This verse says, "Men's hearts failing them." I have heard preachers say this is speaking of the rise of heart attacks and heart disease. It could be, but I think more realistically that it is speaking of people losing heart, giving up, and throwing in the towel. Why? Because they are looking at what is happening in this world. Pastors are watching the youth leave the church. Schools are scheduling events on what was church nights and even on Sundays. Church attendance has become secondary to almost everything. Respect for the gospel and the ministry is at an all-time low, and honestly, we wonder at times if we really are making a difference. Let me say with a resounding *yes*, you are making a difference! It may not be to thousands or even hundreds, but if you can touch one person for Christ, you have made an eternal difference.

Think about Jeremiah. When God called him, He told Jeremiah that nobody would listen, but preach anyway and nobody would be converted but preach anyway. Why, Lord?

It can be disheartening.

Allow me to finish this book with one more story. I told you that I had come to a place where I had doubted everything, as well as God Himself. It was the darkest and driest place I had ever been spiritually, emotionally, and physically. I really wanted to quit, but thankfully, God didn't give up on me. I tried to pray and nothing happened. I was still attending church and doing everything I was supposed to but nothing. One day, after about nine months of nothingness, something happened. I had been given a little puppy. We were living with my in-laws because not only was my spiritual life a mess, no place in our town was hiring. This day, the puppy had gone across the gravel road to play with the neighbor's children. One of the other neighbors, who apparently was late for something, came flying down the road at an unusually fast speed. My pup, Charlie, had heard the car and instinctively knew to get in our yard. He didn't make it and was hit and killed. I was heartbroken. More than that, I was angry. I was angry with the neighbor for driving so fast, because it could have easily been one of the children. I was angry that Charlie had left the yard. I was angry that I hadn't watched him better, but most of all, I was angry at God. One of the few things that I had at that time that brought me some distraction and joy had been taken away. It was one of those "we need to talk now, God" times. I went out in a field and cried out to God. It was enough that we were going through all this because you don't face these times alone; your family goes through it too. It was hard enough going through this, but God's silence made it unbearable. That day, I came through the desert. I cried out, "God, I need you!" and something broke. Suddenly, all of heaven seemed to open up, and I was directly under the opening. I think that there is an old Southern gospel song that says something about being under the spout where the glory comes out. God brought me and my family through that wilderness. Opportunities to minister began to open up. There was an anointing and power in my preaching and ministry that had not been there before. I am reminded of Moses when he ran away from Egypt and the children of Israel going to the promised land. Both had to go through the desert before they found the peace and the presence of God.

So I say to you, when you feel like quitting, and you will, don't. I am praying for you as I write these words. The verse that states, "That we walk by faith and not by sight," became very real to me that summer.

> And let us not be weary in well doing: for
> in due season we shall reap, if we faint not.
> (Galatians 6:9 KJV)

God is with you, and you have got this!

Personal experience or thoughts: _______________________

____

____

____

____

____

____

____

____

____

About the Author

Pastor Brad Reed was born and raised in Southwest Missouri. He accepted Jesus Christ as his personal Savior in a little Pentecostal church in Lebanon, Missouri, in 1984. He was married to his beautiful wife, Joleen, later that same year. They have four married children and, at this time, eight grandchildren. He accepted the call to preach in the fall of 1987 and began his first pastorate in 1989. The Reeds have always been involved in ministry, pastoring four churches in southern Missouri and serving as the district youth director for the Pentecostal Church of God, with whom he is ordained through. The Reeds planted Faith Pentecostal Ministries in 2000 and have been there for twenty-two years. Pastor Reed weaves humor, personal experiences, and the truth of God's Word throughout his teaching, preaching, and writing. His passion is to strengthen and encourage those who are in ministry.